BASED ON A TRUE STORY

IT COULD Easily HAPPEN TO YOU

WRITTEN BY
MICHELE COBB

ISBN: 978-0692884232

Cover and Layout Design: Write On Promotions

A BIG "THANK YOU" TO MY INSPIRATION …

Sundae Cora

Kindra Singleton

Regina Handy

TeNisha Banyard

THIS COULD EASILY BE YOU

A Mother Who's Loved & Lost! Take a walk down memory lane with Michele as she reminisces and shares some private moments with her youngest son (Brannon Mack); before his demise. Embrace yourselves as this memoir gives you a preview into Michele's life as a mother of two handsome young men and the pain of losing her son to gun violence.

Through the eyes of a grieving mother, losing a child is the most hurtful thing I've ever experienced! More often than not, your friends and family will try to sympathize with you by putting themselves in your shoes. They'll strive to seek out ways to offer you some level of comfort by comparing the different losses of their loved ones to yours. Yes, it's a commendable act of kindness! Although it might not be their intention, their comparisons could come across as a way of dismissing my pain. Unbeknownst to them, their actions suggest that I get over my pain by sucking it up and licking my wounds because it's their way of life. Yes, death is a part of life! But until you've lost a child and can walk a mile in my shoes, please, just lend a shoulder or a listening ear. Let him or her know you're there, if needed (only utter the words – if you truly mean it). Know that you will be needed at the most inopportune moment (late nights/early mornings). Be ready for ANYTHING (cussing and fussing included)!

It could

Easily

Happen to

You

~ * ~

June 8, 2016

Things were looking up. After spending three days in the ICU, my son, Brannon, was finally transferred into a regular room. YESSS! My baby was making progress and I was ecstatic. I know it seems crazy, but I was still able to see the bright side of things. Brannon seemed to be in good spirits, considering. He had a lot of visitors that first day and I was happy once everyone left. We spent a lot of time trying to get him comfortable, so he could get some rest. He was scheduled to have surgery the next day. It took a lot of maneuvering to help him find comfort.

During the night, Brannon only took cat naps here and there. Between his cat naps, he and I indulged in some deep conversation, like we had many nights before all of this.

"Brannon," I asked, "have you taken the time to thank God for sparing your life?"

"No Momma," he said, "not yet."

"You were shot nine times," I told him. "None of your major organs were injured. Look, son, there's no time like the present."

Brannon smiled and grabbed my hand. He prayed silently for a few minutes, then said, "Amen."

"Amen, baby!" I exclaimed, deciding not to ask what he prayed about.

We talked about random things. He told me how happy he was that I had found happiness in this crazy world we lived in. He was excited that his girl was coming from out of town to see him, but nervous about the surgery. He told me how he looked forward to moving away soon. He was ready for a fresh start somewhere, where he didn't know a lot of people. My baby was ready to make positive changes in his life, to start anew.

He was tired of the hustle and wanted to make me proud of him on a consistent basis.

Brannon had a big heart and loved his momma! I don't recall getting a lot of sleep that night. I watched a little TV, while Brannon dozed off for a few hours after getting some much-needed pain meds. Then, I drifted off as much as I could in one of those uncomfortable hospital chair beds. By that time, it was in the wee hours of the morning and soon to be daybreak...

~ * ~

June 9, 2016

The next morning, we were awakened by the nurse. She was coming to check in on Brannon's vitals, pain levels, and bandages. Nurses were in and out of Brannon's room all morning. His surgery was scheduled for noon and I had planned to stay with him until it was time.

Brannon seemed a little anxious about the surgery. His girl hadn't arrived at the hospital yet. I tried to comfort him as much as possible.

"Brannon," I told him," the surgery is on your elbow. It will be fine. You know, God has already brought you through being shot nine times."

Brannon just looked at me and didn't say anything. He looked at the clock. "I'm ready to see my girl," Brannon said. "It's almost time."

Unfortunately, the anesthesiologist walked in, ready to take Brannon downstairs. I hugged and kissed Brannon several times, reassuring him that the surgery would go well. I told him it would all be over before he knew it and how much I loved him.

Sadly, my baby never made it out of the recovery room. – It was the worst day of my life.

How could my handsome son of twenty-two years be deceased? Instead of the doctor telling me, "Ms. Mack, Brannon's surgery was a success," I was being told, "Ms. Mack, I'm so sorry. We tried resuscitating Brannon for an hour." How could they lose him in recovery? How? Can somebody tell me how?

Everything became a big blur. I just remember crying out for my baby. I needed him back, right then and there. I couldn't hear anything the doctors were saying. At that point, all I wanted to hear was, "Here's Brannon back. We made a terrible mistake. Here he is, and in one piece." Point blank, period!

My baby had been changing in a positive way. Although he fought the demons inside of him, he tried to break free. Even though Brannon had family and friends who loved him, he often felt alone. As I mentioned earlier, my son and I talked often. I tried to understand him and eventually, I thought I did. It was the lifestyle Brannon had chosen to live. He wasn't brought into this world with a silver spoon in his mouth, but he was loved. He didn't want for much.

My dad had blessed both of my boys with a horse of their own. He taught them each how to ride and care for their horses. They would even attend kids' birthday parties with Daddy and help walk the kids around on horseback. Somewhere along the line, Brannon had roamed down the wrong path and adopted a hard knock lifestyle.

It could *Easily* Happen to You

~ * ~

My family and I often preached to Brannon about his poor judgement. Sometimes, he listened and sometimes, he didn't. Despite getting in his own way, Brannon was a gentle giant with a huge heart and honest by default. Over the years, Brannon had spent a total of three and a half years in jail for three to four different incidents. While in jail, Brannon encountered some horrific circumstances. For instance, there was a scar above his eye, which came from a jail fight, and as you can see, they meant business. Brannon was a very smart and respectful gentleman. He enjoyed having fun and playing practical jokes on everyone. Oh yeah, he had a very strong personality to boot.

Lord, I prayed, *what am I supposed to do without Brannon? Brannon was my baby. He was my second-born son! How am I supposed to live my life without him? What am I supposed to do, Lord? Please answer me, Lord! What am I supposed to do now?*

I honestly wanted to hear from God, to hear His voice! If anyone knew how important Brandon was to me, it was God. I needed Him to tell me how to go on without my son, who had been a part of my heart and life from the last 22 years.

Two weeks after Brannon's funeral, everything had finally calmed down. There were no visitors, less phone calls, and less text and social media messages. I was left alone with my thoughts and nothing but time on my hands. My head was spinning out of control. My mind wandered at record pace. *Where's Brannon?* I thought. *What is he doing?* I couldn't call my baby. I just wanted to hear his voice, smell him, and hug him. I just wanted him.

"Lord, I need you now," I prayed every night. "More than ever! I'm weak, Lord." I didn't want to get out of bed. I was numb to everything and had no motivation to do anything. I knew I still had my oldest son and a family who loved me. They wanted me to keep going, but I didn't know if I could. "Lord, I'm weak!" I cried. "I don't have the strength. I can't do this on my own. Lord, give me Your strength, guide me, carry me, and see me through."

I miss Brannon every moment of every day. I think about him all the time – not a day goes by when I don't, not one. I remembered losing my baby brother in 1991. I thought that was a breaking point in my life, but nope! In 2010, when I lost my dad, I thought I couldn't go on, but nope! It took losing my baby boy to realize the most devastating hurt of my life – losing a child! All kinds of losses hurt, but there are different levels of hurt.

Now, on top of the sleepless nights, anxiety and panic attacks come in. My goodness, when they say it happens in 3's. That's the honest to God truth! From June to August, I had lost my child, my job, and my new car, but I was still standing. It was only by the grace of God!

~ * ~

"Yes, I try to find common ground with everyone, doing everything I can to save some."
Refer to 1 Corinthians 9:22 in your Bible for more clarity.

The above verse is a quote from my morning devotional. It

spoke volumes to me after I lost my son. I knew my son had been murdered due to the heinous crime of gun violence. I feel that God ended my son's earthly life to save his soul and give him eternal life. We all know how important eternal life is!

As I mentioned earlier, my son often felt alone and was very misunderstood. He chose a life for himself that went against God's plan. Brannon was a very intelligent young man (wise beyond his years) and although I'm biased, I'm being honest. When he was a little boy,

Brannon was so bright, but he often got into trouble at school. He was just bored in class, knowing already what the other students were learning. Since kindergarten, Brannon was the class clown and I spent a lot of time meeting with his teachers and principals because of it. I used to tell him that I should've gone fishing on the day he was conceived. Just a little jokey joke! I wouldn't have traded my child or the love I have for him for anything in this world. He was a challenge, but well worth it.

When I think about the spiritual realm, I think about what God has planned for my life. We're all striving to get into Heaven – well, at least I am anyway! So, it's truly a blessing for God to have ended my son's mortal life for his eternal life, That's love! I know we're human and the flesh in us will always want to have our children around. The thought of living a life without them is unbearable. They're supposed to bury us, not the other way around. We forget that God actually gave His only begotten Son to save our souls for eternal life.

I still miss my son every day, but I find peace in knowing that God's in complete control. Although life without Brannon is a constant struggle, I know that Brannon's in a better place now. More often than not, I remind myself that God makes NO mistakes...

It could *Easily* Happen to You

~ * ~

I truly struggled with what to do with Brannon's clothes. He was larger than his older brother and most of his friends. So, that was out! Also, I felt protective over his clothes and didn't want to give anything away to just anybody. So, I thought long and hard about what to do with them. One day, God put it on my heart to have someone do patchwork on a blanket using his clothes. I searched high and low for weeks. Just when I thought I had the perfect person in mind, it didn't work out with them at all. I had to continue my search again. I was referred to someone who could do what I was looking for and was up for the project.

My mom didn't care much for the idea. She thought I should give Brannon's clothes to someone who could wear them and get good use out of them Well, I didn't want to do that. I felt like that wasn't enough. I wanted to preserve his clothes and make them a keepsake. I wanted something people could admire and cherish their memories of him. I had a few sample blankets made using Brannon's clothes and the seamstress did such an awesome job. She exceeded my expectations and did such phenomenal work with so much love.

For one of the blankets, the seamstress used one of the

shirts I used to love seeing Brannon wear. I found the perfect fabric to match the shirt and Brannon's personality. Everything came together nicely. When I saw the blanket for the first time, it made me emotional.

Now, when I lay down at night, I reach for my blanket and I can feel my son's big bear hug. Each time I use the blanket, it brings me such comfort and solace. It even feels like I can get into a deeper realm of sleep. I would dream and remember my dreams in the morning. This was something I was never able to do in the past.

Thank God! God is good all the time... and all the time, God is good! God truly moved mountains in my life. He introduced me to new people, who assisted me in ways they didn't even realize. I found out about an opportunity to mentor young men in my own hometown. It was music to my ears. I had so much information to share with them!

~ * ~

Sometimes, I feel like I did my boys a great injustice when I divorced their father. They were still young and at impressionable stages in their lives. My parents were a phenomenal help to me, and my dad was an awesome role model.

The boys really looked up to my dad a great deal.

My parents were Christians and active in the church. I grew up in the church from when I was a little girl, but I lost my way after my brother died. He was in his early 20s when he passed away and I spent a long time being angry with God. Eventually, I found my way back to Him and the church.

Society often says, "A woman cannot raise a man!" I agree with this statement to a degree. A woman probably "cannot" raise a man on her own, but with her village, God's grace, and His mercy, she can! Life is all about what you make of it and by keeping God first, you create a divine opportunity.

Although my parents took my boys to church with them, I wish my sons had seen me attending church more often. If they had, I think my boys would've viewed me in a more positive light and as more of a God-fearing woman. I love the Lord with all my might! Unfortunately, it took such tremendous loss to awaken me and bring me closer to Him. I'm ever so grateful to God for His undying and unwavering love! If it wasn't for God's strength, I'd still be in such a deep dark place. God is so good... and to God be the glory!

~ * ~

It's so funny how life works – not funny ha-ha, but funny in a peculiar way. Sometimes, when you think long and hard about a person, God will have that person call you or you'll see them. Life is a journey filled with predestined plans mapped out by God. Sometimes, we take the right roads, and sometimes, we don't. God allows us to decide which route we're going to take. Prayerfully, we're choosing the route that God's on, so He can lead us to our destinies!

Take this book for instance. Never in a million years did I ever think I would write a book. As a little girl, I always enjoyed reading and writing. Once upon a time, I had planned to pursue a career as a journalist but ended up on a different path– one filled with numbers. I love working with numbers, but God must've already had this book predestined for my life. Since Brannon's death, I constantly said I wanted to be his voice. Brannon's story needed to be heard, but I just had no idea how. I didn't know that I would have this huge of a platform to tell my son's story. I can't praise God enough. To God be the glory! He truly moves in mysterious ways.

"Be strong and courageous. Do not be afraid or terrified because of them, for the LORD your God goes with you; He will

never leave you or forsake you" (Deuteronomy 31:6).

~ * ~

One morning, I was reminiscing of Brannon and thought of a specific conversation we had had years ago. A dear loved one of ours had received a horrific jail sentence. I don't think Brannon was quite a teenager yet.

My son asked me, "Do you believe all the terrible things they're saying on the news about A.J.?"

"No," I exclaimed. "I don't agree with the media coverage or any of the reports about him. We know –A.J. is a great person with a big heart. The media totally ridiculed and demeaned his character."

"Yeah, but sometimes good people make bad decisions," said Brannon. "That doesn't make them bad people."

From the mouth of babes, I thought. I was totally surprised, but proud of my son's words. I had always known that my baby was wise beyond his years, and our conversation was proof of that. It's probably surprising to most, but Brannon thought deeply about his words before speaking them. If only Brannon could've seen in himself what I saw in him. He was always a confident young man and very tech savvy with a lust for life. He had such great potential!

It's so puzzling to me. No matter how often I spoke life into him, society and the streets still managed to pique his interest and hold his attention. It's so crazy how the streets glamorize material things and grasp such a hold on our youth. We must really speak life into our children before they leave the womb and well into adulthood It truly starts with us and I'm a firm believer of that. Somewhere along the line, I lost sight of that with my own child. Understand me when I say, I was always there for both my boys. Sure, we had some bumps and bruises along the way. There were times I'm not so proud of and days when I had to rob Peter to pay

Paul. However, with God's grace and mercy, He, got us through!

Meanwhile, the times when I fretted the most were the times when I spared the rod and spoiled the child. Regretfully, I wasn't always as stern and firm as I could've been when disciplining the boys. As Brannon got older, he became angrier. Twice, I had him go to counseling, but Brannon never completed all of the sessions. We did have some great times and those outweighed the bad. My boys and I watched movies together all the time. We would break into a dance session and sing along with the movie. Brannon was very fond of the movie, *White Chicks,* and he could sing the songs word for word.

~ * ~

The Lord never ceases to amaze me. There's power in prayer! We must exercise faith and trust in His Word. I firmly believe our prayer life and personal relationship with God will set the tone for us. It is important to believe in God and

His power to answer our prayers, especially because life is so unpredictable.

Sometimes, the paths we choose will cause us to make some tough decisions. There will be times when we must realize that some people in our circle are at different points in their lives and may not understand our journey. Unfortunately, this could mean having to separate ourselves from certain people, places, and things. Otherwise, we could find ourselves in situations that could deter us and take us off course. Poor judgement could compromise your fate. It could put us in the wrong place at the wrong time.

We can be introduced to new people with ulterior motives and ill-willed intentions. As much as we'd like for the world to be peaceful and for everyone to love one another, there are some cruel and hateful posers that exist. Posers can appear beautiful on the exterior, while dying a slow death within. Someone can take you off of your path in the blink of an eye, especially if you lose sight of God's discernment. There's an infamous quote that states, "When someone shows you who they are, believe them."

Sometimes, God can use situation to enforce His will for our lives. We must recognize the signs and know how to be still long enough to hear His voice. Whenever something seems impossible, the Lord will make a way out of no way!

~ * ~

God truly works in mysterious ways! He will put things on our hearts and in our minds to lead us towards actions that can impact lives. It's up to us to listen and be obedient. My family and friends know that I'm a private person.

It isn't normal for me to be open and transparent to a bunch of strangers. I made a choice to follow God's nudge and to utilize the platform that was placed before me. I knew there was something brewing that was larger than myself or anyone else. I NEED FOR BRANNON'S VOICE TO BE HEARD.

There are young men out there who need to understand the amount of hurt their parents experience when their lives are taken... and so MALICIOUSLY, if I might add.

It's not about you or me. It's about our youth, OUR YOUNG MEN. I'm almost certain that there are some young men and women, who may feel as though the streets love them more than their own family, or that they're in it too deep. They believe there's no turning back now. Well, THEY'RE WRONG!

Uneasiness and loneliness are all works of the enemy. He wants you to continue feeling that way. He wants to isolate you and steer you away from your family. Your family LOVES and ACCEPTS you as you are without question. You are great and of GREAT stock! Your minds are like machines that produce information and ideas daily! You possess so much potential and can be ANYTHING or ANYONE you set your mind to be. The world is your oyster, so stop allowing the enemy to hold you down. Show the world what you have to offer. TAKE back your POWER and let that setback be the preface to your COME UP. You can OVERCOME!

Even though we're strangers, I want each of you to trust and believe that I LOVE

YOU. Most importantly, GOD LOVES YOU! So, be the best version of yourselves that you can be... and GOD SPEED!

www.ingramcontent.com/pod-product-compliance
Lightning Source LLC
Chambersburg PA
CBHW071734020426
42331CB00008B/2028